The Untethered
Elephant

How to Reshape Memories to
Increase Possibility

Max Gallegos

Published in Austin, Texas

Visit www.fearlesscoachingwithmax.com

Layout and design by Mike Ivy, www.m8yos.com

Library of Congress Control Number: 2023924546

ISBN: 979-8-9893388-1-8

The Untethered Elephant

Table of Contents

Foreword

Dear reader,

After I read the original version of this book I was so excited about the effectiveness of the subtle shifts of viewpoint it afforded me that I was compelled to begin sharing this information with people near to me. However, it turned out I wasn't very good at verbally conveying the information I received from this book. People would immediately associate the concepts I attempted to explain with other forms of memory work they had heard of before. I couldn't seem to adequately describe the difference to them. This work was too gentle and personal to be put into a short passing conversation. It had to be read. I became eager for Max to complete the work so that I could simply place the message into people's hands and trust that it would find a place in their heart like it had in mine.

We often scorn or dismiss subtle shifts. People want clear effective action right here right now. But as we all know deep down, real change and real success are determined by small actions. Any physical therapist would confirm that no one gets strong from one day of tremendous exercise, yet lives are transformed by gentle stretches done regularly. Artists know that songs, poems and paintings are made up of one note, word and mark at a time, and that tiny changes in the quality of those things will significantly transform the completed work. Even one note being different can give a song the feeling of tension or of peace. So don't scorn the small stuff.

The work described in this book is about looking at those dissonant notes in the song of our life and considering that maybe they could be shifted just a half-step to afford us more harmony. Yet describing it as such still sounds too dramatic to me. Maybe it's more like going hours on an airplane flight then suddenly realizing with relief that the seat can recline just a little bit. I'm sure you'll find your own best metaphor. I trust that the words in this book will continue to find receptive hearts ready to gently transform and find that little bit of extra room to stretch and breathe.

With love and joy,
Max's Son

Introduction

My reason for writing this book is the ideas within it are useful like a hammer or a saw. You wouldn't use either of those tools for the same job nor for every job, but when you need a hammer or a saw, nothing else will do. This book is less about creating positive memories and more about becoming a mental meteorologist. It is the clouds of memories in the sky of our mind which control our mental weather patterns and ultimately how we navigate our daily lives. It is also about reclaiming and harnessing the energy wasted on dysfunctional relationships trapped by memories of failure, confusion, shame, and blame.

As it can be for many of us, our existence is hijacked by the memories that keep us from being fully present. The memories which keep you from being fully present are those which make you hold on to them and ask:

"What if . . . ?" or;

"If I'd done such and such, would my life be different now?"

You are not actually using your senses to record a moment in time like some organic video recorder. It is your active imagination that creates memories. It is the same imagination you used as a little girl or boy to creatively imagine and act out tea parties with stuffed animals or build forts with imaginary soldiers. It is playful and active. It engages all your senses. Using your imagination (some may call it your active imagination) to reshape your memories cuts the ropes that restrict you from fully engaging in your life. These are the memories that limit you from being fully present. They limit your possibilities and hinder your evolution. The memories significant and in need of reshaping are those which define you in ways which are limiting and keep you in the same track or path which makes you believe your life can't change. Remember, memories are less an exact recording of a moment in time and more a cloud containing wisps of images and feelings experienced long ago. It is what is captured after your active imagination files the "recording" away.

What reshaping memories is not:

- This is not about writing a new story of your life.

- This is not about seeking revenge or giving someone a piece of your mind.

- This is not about putting someone in his/her place.

- This is not about being right or better than.

What reshaping memories is about:

- It is about unlocking the possibilities which up until now have had boundaries and limitations set by those controlling memories.

- It is about injecting wisdom and clarity into your past.

- It is about giving you back the power to choose your path.

Controlling memories keep you stuck in the past, tied to someone else's bad behavior, tethered by your hurt and pain, and lost in the swamp of the dissatisfied mind, which means you are not fully present to what is happening in your life now. This is not magic. This is not about becoming a Shaman. This does not replace your therapist or medical prescriptions. This does not take the place of reconciling relationships when safe and appropriate.

Please consider there may be other learning, journeys, or insights that need to happen after you've done some memory reshaping. You may need to reshape a memory a few times to set the reshaped memory in place. There may be other work you need to do to reconnect with your childlike, playful mind. When done right, it just feels like your heart has become unburdened. It is easier to breathe, and you can think about that reshaped memory without the previous negative emotional charge because it provides a new way of seeing the world and yourself. You will navigate differently through the world. The sky in your mind has fewer gray clouds blocking the sun of clarity shining on a life of expanding possibility. That is what reshaping memories will do for your life: increase possibility. It is increased possibility that allows you to see how some memories have restricted your vision and limited your choices.

Consider this, when elephants are young, circus animal trainers will tie a rope or chain around a leg and tether it to a peg in the ground strong enough to hold the young animal. Once the elephant has grown, the animal does not try to escape although it is now big and strong enough to pull any peg or stake from the ground. It's only the memory of the chain as a young elephant that keeps the elephant from escaping. In the same way, you are kept from escaping memories which you have determined restrict your movement.

Me in a very small nutshell:

My personal journey has taken me down many paths of spiritual and personal development. I've meditated until bored out of my mind and attempted to use yogic powers to dissolve clouds. My lack of focus for spiritual development is overshadowed by my ability to step into the flow state while painting or doing photography. None of this is a badge of authorship for this or any other book. Yet, here we are, and here I am putting words on paper about my personal experience as I think others could benefit from what I've done. It isn't hard. It's not magical. It doesn't need a licensed professional holding your hand to uncover your pearl of wisdom and clarity. The requirement is simple enough: pick some significant memories that continue to trouble you, those which are like a barking dog in your neighborhood in the middle of the night that just won't stop barking. If you choose to reshape those significant memories, it's like waking up fully and realizing that it was your dog barking all along and all you needed to do was bring him indoors so he can sleep at the foot of your bed. In picking memories to reshape, it may be enough to say to yourself this memory continues to bother me.

1
Reality and Possibility

"It might be helpful if we imagine reality as a field of possibility. Every moment potentially opens into an unknown number of possibilities. Which future possibilities actually open for us are determined, at least partially, by our current understanding of reality."

Jeff Carreira

Our current understanding of reality is part and parcel of our memories. The memories we hold on to reflect our understanding of reality and determine the possibilities open to us.

Early on in my studies to delve into active dreaming and shamanic practices, I was disappointed at not finding practical ways to improve my daily existence. This was a good thing. It led me to experiment. It led me to search for other books and teachers with new and unorthodox ways of traversing the dreamworld and non-ordinary reality. To reshape your memories, you don't have to meditate or breathe a certain way. You don't have to listen to the beating of a drum. You don't have to do guided imagery or meditation. You don't need to retrieve any part of your soul. You don't need to change religious or spiritual beliefs. You just need to bring up a memory and have the

9

courage to reshape it. Memories in need of reshaping are not those you have to seek therapy for or in any way haunt you. They seem to be very quietly and inconspicuously passing in the sky of your mind like a cloud or floating on the river in the back of your mind, bobbing up and down like missed boats of opportunity. Although they don't seem to restrict you from getting downstream to real, true opportunity, they do limit how far you can travel.

2
An Expanded View of Your Personal Universe

*"Our memories are constructive. They're reconstructive. Memory works ...
like a Wikipedia page; you can go in there and change it, but so can other
people."*

Professor Elizabeth Loftus

Imagine an expanded view of your life is like a family tree or genealogy map. Rather than junctions where your ancestors are, there are junctions where you've made a choice. I call these choice points. These choice points lead to where you are in your life today. Now imagine that at each of those choice points is where you in an alternate universe made a different choice. That alternate you is at a different place in life because of choosing differently. All those choice points not only give rise to different choices by alternate selves, but also provide you opportunity to reconnect with those choices via your memory. All the positive energy and possibilities that your alternate selves enjoyed can be reclaimed for yourself. The impact will be felt across your personal universe and also influence the universe of your alternate selves. It will shift your current life path trajectory. You may not be able to go back in time and change your ancestor's family tree, but you can go back and change your memory tree. Different choices reveal different outcomes and therefore alter your path.

Memory reshaping works not because of alternate selves or coming to believe in a quantum physics view of the universe. It works because memories are a major part of our current reality and influence how we see ourselves and the world. They are the filter through which we view the world. Memory reshaping works because memories are malleable. A reshaped memory changes the filter through which you see the world and shifts how you respond to the world. Your path realigns with this new mental orientation. Although it is difficult to unburden yourself from memories which keep you stuck, memories are not an exact replica or digital recording of your experience. They are a conglomeration of deep feelings and a snapshot of what seemed most important to capture at that time. That vague mental construct is malleable. It can be reshaped. Your orientation in the world and the guiding thoughts for how you respond to the world are shaped by memories. In essence, the internal clothes you wear are your memories. Just as you respond differently to the world if you put on a business suit or slip into a red-carpet dress, you respond in new ways to your environment with new memories.

3

Addressing Memory Assumptions & Myths

"Any event, no matter how important, emotional or traumatic it may seem, can be forgotten, misremembered, or even be fictitious."

Dr. Julia Shaw

Memory, Dreams and Reality

I believe memories are more closely related to dreams than actual reality. Although you may travel through your dreams with your everyday ideas of what is possible, in fact, other rules apply. You don't necessarily have to have a lucid dream to understand or experience this. Dreaming is its own reality. Dreams have messages related to your daily existence, yet are often discounted with the phrase, it's only a dream. This misunderstanding of dreams and the wealth of wisdom and learning made available in those nightly journeys, cuts off individuals from a natural source of guidance and inspiration. Hopefully, you've noticed memories have a dreamlike quality. Dreams reveal a constant effort by our dreaming self to reach us, to get our attention. It is the part of us that never tires of providing insight and direction, unfortunately few of us are trained to listen. I believe we do ourselves a disservice by treating memories as a movie of a moment from our daily existence. We would be better served by treating memories like a dream, a dream to be recalled and reshaped for personal benefit.

What Does It Mean to be Whole?

The question may be more clear and easier to answer if we think of it as what causes a person to be out of balance? One of the goals of this book is to help individuals find wholeness. Wholeness is balance. All the pieces that make up a human being may become out of balance. This happens quite naturally, and it is not my intent to uncover how this comes to be. Once out of balance, it is not only uncomfortable but also quite difficult to determine what is out of balance and what can be done to correct the imbalance. If you find you are out of balance, it may just seem like you woke up on the wrong side of the bed or you seem to be somewhat on edge. There are many ways you can feel that things aren't quite right in your life. Not all of these indicate you are out of balance. It may be your intuition sending you a message as to what needs your attention. Memories can be a constant anchor to maintain your imbalance. If, for whatever reason, you are hanging on to memories as if they cannot be changed or are sacred to your existence, hopefully by the end of this book you will see the wisdom in reshaping memories to help restore you to balance.

The Playful, No-limit Mind

Let's take a journey back to when your imagination was unlimited. Let's look at what you did as a child once you discovered you could imagine what you wanted in your life. Let's engage with your younger self that believed acting with intent and selfish purpose was enough to engage in the world. Let's look at your early memories of Play. At what age do you remember playing? I'm talking about playing where you've made up the rules. This is not about when a parent has played peek-a-boo with you. This is when you first remember going outside or into your bedroom and rather than being bored, you made up your own little world with invisible people, talking stuffed animals, and scenarios possibly inspired by stories read to you but self-created and now taking on your own twists and turns. Maybe you stepped into a story read to you by your mother or father.

Perhaps you were a king or queen, and your stuffed animals or dolls, or figurines were your subjects. Did you tell your parents about your invisible friends? Did you question what you experienced? In your imagination, did you question that Johnny or Suzie, your invisible friends, could not be seen by others? Are those memories any less real than the ones you can recall about being in school with other children like yourself; physically present and self-aware?

Are Memories Sacred?

I want to briefly address the question of the sacredness of memories. In other words, should memories not be tampered with? I believe this is a valid topic as the psychological community holds the reins to memories and addresses troubling memories because the belief is that only psychological methods can resolve them in any helpful way. I've had my fair share of counseling and psychological therapy. Just as in any other profession, there are good therapists and not so good therapists. Underlying the therapeutic model is an unstated view of memories as if they are sacred, set in stone, and in need of professional help. This is despite the numerous studies conducted which reveal the amorphous nature of our mental constructs. If memories are viewed for their true nature and not as some religious, unchanging myth, we come to realize there is less a solid form but only a memory made more solid by revisiting it throughout our lives. Memory is not a video that resides in our mental databanks like a computer intentionally limiting our progress and evolution. A memory maintains its shape because we conduct touchups of the paint on the walls of every room where a memory is held and then replay it in what we have come to believe is its original form. We ignore the part we play in maintaining bothersome memories. We allow its formless and translucent nature to be elevated to the status as sacred while ignoring our hand holding the paint brush and our finger on the replay button. In that room where the memory is held with all the things which make it seem solid, there also stands the creator, the dreamer, you. You can take any memory without the approval of another person and reshape it. The sacredness of a memory comes from you. Reshaping a memory does not violate any unstated religious or psychological law. What it does is put the power back into the hands of the maker of the memory. Underlying how a memory appears to you is the fact that you have chosen how to remember it. You can choose differently.

Understand that I am not advocating using memory

reshaping on traumatic memories. Once PTSD and other life-altering aspects from a traumatic experience are involved, the memory is less a choice and more an emotional, psychological, and sometimes physical injury that pierces the soul, the very foundation of being human and whole. Using memory reshaping for those traumatic experiences would be like getting your car washed when you need a new carburetor. A traumatic memory requires help from a licensed professional specializing in the traumatic experience that has affected your life. When you try to push away or block out traumatic memories, they seem to become more real and rooted. In other words, traumatic memories are not appropriate for the reshaping process.

4
The Energy of Memory

Thought is energy, energy is vibrations, and vibrations attract the same vibrations.

Ana Pat

Before I provide the steps to reshape a memory I want to talk about the energy of memory. To understand the energy of memory, it's important to know that memory is a nexus connecting thoughts, behaviors, life-trajectory, self-concept, and relationships from the inception of the memory. There are no dead memories. In other words, memories continue to have a half-life like radioactive material. It is not always the case that the further you move away from the point a memory is captured the less effect it has. The continuing effects caused to the areas mentioned above reveals a memory's energy. Consider that a memory is a thought. Think of it like a thought revisited. Your response to that memory to the degree the areas mentioned reveals its energy level. Think of those situations to be a window you look through as you begin a new relationship or embark on a new career. What are those memories that come to mind when you complete the sentences below?

I wish I'd never said _____ to my parent, friend, spouse, child.

If I could only go back to this point in time when _____ happened, I would make a more positive decision.

Although _____ has passed away, I wish I had acted differently that time when _____ happened.

I wonder what my life would be like now if I had not made the decision to _____.

Who am I if I no longer believe I failed at _____?

Who am I if I no longer think I am a victim because of what happened with _____?

Imagine within each one of us is an exchange where energy is traded, and part of that exchange is where memories trade energy for possibility. The energy of a memory affects our actions, thoughts, and possibility of what we may become.

5

How to Reshape a Memory

1. Find a quiet location where you can be undisturbed.

2. You can be seated with your back straight or lying down on your back.

3. Simple centering breathing: take 3 deep breaths through your nose and release each breath through your mouth.

4. State your intent: I desire to be free from the constraints contained in this memory.

5. Revisit the memory as you remember it and write it down in your journal.

6. Now revisit the memory again and ask the questions below.

When you think about the memory you want to reshape, where does it feel like it resides in your body? Do you have a sense that it's on the left or right side? Is it behind your ribs? Is it in your thigh or another muscle? Does it reside in your gut? Is it in one of your organs? Is it behind your eyes? Where does it feel like it resides in your body when you think about it? Does it have a feeling of hardness or softness? Does it evoke a color? Red? Green? Black? Does it seem to be smooth or have a prickly feeling like a cactus? Do you get the sense that it has some heat to it or coldness? Feel those senses that come to you; location, color, texture, temperature, etc. Do you have any smell that comes to you? Do you feel any vibration or hum?

Place a hand on the part of your body where you get a sense of where that memory resides. Imagine you can feel all those qualities of the memory under your hand; hot/cold, hard/soft, texture, color, vibration, sound, etc.? Do you have a sense of the shape of that memory under your hand? Is it circular like a ball or does it have edges and sides like something geometric? Allow those sensations to be just under your hand without any judgment or rejection.

7. Write all the characteristics of the memory you discovered in your journal.

Repeat this phrase after recording in your journal: I desire to be free from the constraints and limitations to my growth and possibilities contained in this memory.

8. Reshape the memory as directed below:

Now reshape the memory by writing it in your journal as you wish it to be. Allow it to evolve and reveal itself with as little control as possible. In other words, let the memory almost write itself. What does your imagination create, knowing that what you have held onto for whatever length of time needs to change? Record it in your journal with as much detail as you can.

Look at my reshaped memories in the book to get clarity on how to reshape a memory. Notice that my responses and reactions are changed. Those are the things that I had the power to change when those memories were originally captured. Memory reshaping is in some ways self-development and self-realization. It is in a sense placing a wiser self into your personal experience in the past. It is almost as if you are answering the question, if I could go back in time when a certain thing happened how would I respond or how would it be different? Although it does not change what happened, on an unseen level (whether quantum, psychological, or spiritual) a change takes place. Energetically, a change has taken place that is significant. Recouping the energy of possibility and altering your life path is the goal.

Take the time after recording the reshaped memory in your journal to take 3 deep breaths in through your nose and out through your mouth. Now sense where the reshaped memory exists in your body. Besides location, what other characteristics of the memory have changed? Color? Shape? Texture? Temperature? Softness? Etc.? Feel that reshaped memory under your hand.

9. Write all the characteristics of the reshaped memory in your journal.

Repeat this phrase after recording it in your journal:

I accept all of the new possibilities this reshaped memory provides to my growth and evolution.

6
Examples of Reshaped Memories

"Even the precious memories of our childhood can actually be shaped and reshaped like a ball of clay."

Dr. Julia Shaw

1. Not Divorcing My First Wife

Why this memory was chosen:

Although the time leading up to and after the divorce is quite foggy, I've never stopped loving my first wife and have always felt that somehow if we had not gotten divorced it would have all worked itself out. So, choosing this memory is really "what if I had not gotten divorced?" You can see from my reshaping that deep down in some part of me I realized that there were still underlying issues.

Memory:

I was married to my first wife for a little over seven years. There are many reasons it fell apart, and it was painful divorce. It seemed that the time leading up to the divorce and at least for the year after the divorce that I was on a runaway train. I look back, and I don't see any way that I could have stopped the wheels from turning. What I remember most is my broken heart and the lingering feeling that we should not have gotten divorced. It is quite easy to remember that pain and longing.

Reshaping:

I go back into the memory and reshape it by connecting with the alternate self that did not divorce. Somehow the hard feelings are patched up. I see us reconciling and being more deeply connected as a couple. I also imagine that we had another child, a girl, four years after our son was born. I continue in my role as a sales trainer and end up working in Arizona for a large corporation. Eventually, my wife and I do divorce later in our marriage.

Note: This reshaping is not to justify to myself that we would have gotten divorced later. It is a quite healthy confirmation that despite the divorce pain, shame, and suffering that within some part of me there is hidden insight that would have revealed itself at some point. Also note that you should trust your active imagination in the reshaping process to create a memory which aligns with your wholeness.

2. Undoing My Second Marriage

Why this memory was chosen:

The marriage to my second wife was quite dysfunctional. I can't imagine that the eighteen-year marriage and all that transpired would be easy to gather all the memories that would need to be reshaped. Instead, I've chosen to reshape a memory of when that path began. My experiment is to show that reshaping the memory of beginning on a path somehow unravels this relationship. Of course, I can reshape any memories from this relationship in the future that continue to trouble me.

Memory:

I rush into another marriage although I am aware of many red flags about my girlfriend's past. I was proud of myself for finding a younger woman that would accept my love and affection. Even after many months of a long-distance relationship where more red flags were raised, I flew to her city to propose. From that point on, I continued to ignore the red flags and made the huge assumption that I could love this woman enough to heal her damaged past. It was only until 18 years later that I felt brave enough to get divorced and lay down my savior's cape and begin to live in a healthy way.

Reshaping:

In my mind, I imagine the time when I flew to the city where she lived to propose. I have clarity about my own needs, confusion, and delusions. Rather than proposing, I bless her for pursuing an acting career. I tell her to continue to follow her dream of being a great actor. I can see the hurt in her eyes but realize the wisdom of what I'm saying, and that is the healthiest thing for both of us. I fly back home with the realization that my need to be a martyr is crippling and that I can live differently without grasping, chasing, and obsessing over another person.

3. Confronting Gaslighters

Why this memory was chosen:

Of all my experiences where someone has used the smokescreen of gaslighting, this is the experience that troubles me most. Did I misunderstand? Did I create the impossible promise in my own mind, hoping to twist my father's financial arm? This memory has resulted in my questioning my own memory of the event and in some way my own sanity. It clearly needs a makeover.

Memory:

I am in junior college. I am a chemistry major and believe I want to follow in my father's footsteps and go to medical school. I share this with my father and my stepmother. My father tells me in front of my stepmother that if I get straight A's and get accepted into the state university system that he will pay my tuition. I do get straight A's and after applying to the state university system, I receive a letter of acceptance. I take a copy of my final grades and the letter of acceptance to my father. I show him the documents. My stepmother is sitting on the couch nearby. My father says this is great news and then asks how I will be paying for my tuition. I remind him of what he told me, and he says he never said that. I look over at my stepmother, and she won't lift her eyes to look at me.

Reshaping:

I step back into this memory and share my good news. As before, my father asks how I will pay for tuition. I remind him of his promise, and he says he never said that. I let him know that I did not imagine that conversation and that I would not have made it up to force his hand. Rather than dropping out of school, I let him know that I will go to the university and meet with university financial aid folks and figure out how to get tuition paid even if it means starting at a later semester. I let him know I will be glad to help out in his office until I start school again. A new memory and energy path is created.

4. Blindsided Taken Out of the Will

Why this memory was chosen:

I've never felt that love for my father was because of his wealth and the possibility that I would inherit some portion of his estate. It felt very personal when he announced that I was taken out of his will. It was almost like he was saying you are no longer my son. The year or two prior to that, I felt our relationship was the best it had ever been. I felt close to him. Our bond seemed stronger than it had ever been. Being taken out of the will made me question what I imagined our relationship was.

Memory:

I've come to visit my father. In my mind, it was a great visit – lots of good dialogue and heart-to-heart talks. He insists on driving me to the airport for the return trip home. A few minutes from the airport, he informs me that he and my stepmother signed documents to take me out of the will. His reason is he does not approve of who I voted for in the last presidential election, which was several years prior. I am saddened by this and begin to cry.

Reshaping:

My father informs me a few minutes before dropping me off at the airport that I am no longer in his will. I tell him the following:

"It's your money to do with as you please. Just know that I've done nothing wrong. There's no biblical justification for what you are doing. Love as defined in the Bible does not support what you are doing. To give away my inheritance is your personal choice, not a God thing. It makes me sad. It's petty. I will pray for you to get back in your right mind. You've given me so many examples as to how NOT to be a father to my own son, and I thank you for that because that makes me a better father to him."

7
The Test

Does anything significant change after memory reshaping? Does the reshaped memory become predominate over the original memory? Does life take an alternate path after memory reshaping? These are the main questions you may be asking. If these questions cannot be answered in the affirmative, then there really is little reason to reshape memories. I want to put a reshaped memory to the test as to whether reshaping made a difference. For this test, I'll be looking specifically at reshaped memory #3 above and provide the insights I came to understand during each week.

6-Week Test of a Reshaped Memory

I offered to assist my stepmother with organizing and dispersing of random clutter my father had collected over half a century. It felt important for me to do this prior to his passing. So, I committed to six weeks in the old homestead.

As I stood in line to board the plane, I wondered if the usual underlying tension would still be there. The tension that felt like a red lightbulb in the back of my mind ready to be turned on at any second, signaling that I was stepping into a gaslighting false reality. After all, these people had been with me in moments where my reality was crushed. I knew if I arrived and found the decades old tension intact that memory reshaping was less a tool and merely a mind game not worth the effort. Now that I've reshaped some of my memories of them, would I feel any different being back in the presence of these people?

Week 1

Here we are at the end of week one. Not only am I on task to clear out shelves and drawers and desks, but my flight response has not been triggered which has been a common reaction in the past. Everything, including familiar behaviors on the part of family members, seems to be encased in a soft invisible barrier. The hard edges of personalities and rooms with uncomfortable memories seem to be drained of any possibility of triggering me again. I realize these people have no power over me, and the only thing that is different with this visit is the memory which was reshaped. There now seems to be the possibility that going forward, our relationships can be healthier because I am different.

Week 2

My underlying belief about what happened in my original memory was that my life took a negative turn. I held the thought that I was on a positive path to become a doctor, and that path was yanked out from under me. I saw myself as a victim and blamed my father and stepmother for the negative trajectory of my life. I believed I was powerless in that moment. I did not own my response as significant. There were so many ways I could have responded but I fell right back into a reactive mode that I had used many times in my life. I acted as if the only response was to take an entirely different path. My viewpoint was that of being the Phoenix that could rise from the ashes. Seeing myself in that way made me feel powerful and in control. I could not see that that way of seeing myself was in fact limiting in so many ways. I did not seek guidance from anyone but portrayed myself to family and friends as having been wronged. I wonder now what I would have done if I had simply asked trusted people in my life what would they have done if that had happened to them. That would have been the only way my reactive mind could have seen an alternative. I wonder if I could have grasped a different viewpoint and made a different choice. At least with the memory reshaped, I can take advantage of the benefits of setting aside the negative aftereffects of that extreme choice. It feels satisfying now to be able to say to myself, I took that negative turn at that time. I made the choice, and it was not forced upon me. Ultimately, I am accountable and responsible for how I respond. There are always many choices and possibilities.

Week 3

I find myself thinking of all the positive things my father and stepmother did for me during the years I lived with them. The most significant thing seems to be that I am not holding onto pain or any negative emotion when I engage in conversation or interact in any way. My previous way of being around them involved being guarded to not be taken advantage of or misled. That way of protecting myself is absent. Each of them seems to be different somehow, and yet I know it is because I am different and that I'm no longer looking at them through any kind of filter of distrust and anger. It may be the first time that I am seeing them for who they truly are rather than what I expect them to be.

Week 4

There are junctures in our lives that lead to significant

events. Because of that decision to dislodge myself from school and reinvent myself, it eventually led to my returning to the American Southwest where I got married and had a son. I am confident that the medical professional life I hoped for would have solidified my putting down roots, but probably not in the Southwest. Ultimately, the cut and run reaction to the gaslighting I encountered led to relocating, marriage, and a child. My relationship with my son is my most treasured relationship. Although I would not change the critical path of my life and what I have in it today, the lingering negative elements itching in the back of my mind needed to be reshaped so I could open to more compassionate relationships and clear perceptions of others. I don't believe merely trying to see that original memory in a more positive light would have significantly changed my perception of others and spurred any deep insights.

Week 5

Although I've been feeling accepting and compassionate toward my father and stepmother these past few weeks, I cannot deny that when my half-siblings are in the picture that distrust creeps in. I cannot pinpoint any memory, but I realize that however my half-siblings are interacted with, I see it as negative and believe it confirms that my father and stepmother cannot be trusted. This is a positive realization because I did not think memory reshaping would solve every problem nor that it could have global impact in someone's relationship universe. I'm not surprised, but I do recognize the value in reshaping to reveal other patterns and negative characteristics worth looking into. The problem was not actually the actions of my father or stepmother as I previously believed. The problem was my own negative thoughts. There must be a memory which can be reshaped to bring about a positive change to this lingering way of viewing my half-siblings.

Week 6

My habitual reaction to being gaslighted was virtually unseen by me at the time I was told no promise was made for financial assistance for school. The assumptions I jumped to were seen as the natural, obvious solution to the promise of tuition being taken away. That extreme way of reacting to my father and stepmother was the routine way I would react to almost everything they did. I find as I engage with them during this six-weeks, there is no immediate way that I respond. The usual "go-to" response seems to just be an empty container. So, in conversations with them now, I am listening with an openness and true desire to understand. My heart goes out to them in a way it never has before. I know my father's life growing up was not easy. My stepmother had to be strong to stay in the marriage. I was only a small part of their very complicated life together. My father is not a bad man for going back on his promise of paying tuition. He was unable to be honest about his changed decision. Understanding this does not justify it. Understanding this reveals how human and flawed he is. For whatever reason, his denial of making the promise was easier than telling the truth and possibly what was modeled to him growing up.

What testing this reshaped memory revealed:

I suffered a failure of imagination. I did not give myself the opportunity to redeem the situation. I was impatient and put unnecessary time constraints on myself. In other words, I felt I needed to decide immediately rather than seeking wise counsel and feedback from others. My perception of the event was that it was negative rather than viewing it as an opportunity. I felt I had been wronged and held that belief like a badge of honor.

8
Summary

Most often the simple solution is best. The ways and means we've gathered over the years to navigate the world don't necessarily need to be swapped for a new system. We do, however, need specific tools for specific jobs. Memory reshaping is a simple tool and doesn't require upending any long-held beliefs. Using memory reshaping does require you have an open mind about memories and the energy contained in them.

As I've stated previously, memories can hijack our existence such that we are kept from being fully present. We can be kept in these never-ending loops wondering what could be different rather than taking control and creating the life we want. As children, we naturally use our active imaginations to create what we desire, but as we age, we are not taught how to use active imagination in ways to improve our lives. Using active imagination as a child is never truly lost. As we age, it is merely misunderstood how it relates to memories. Once we understand that many memories are controlling in our lives, we have the tools to reshape them and increase our possibilities for navigating differently without the limitations of the controlling memories.

There is no reason to remain tethered to restrictive memories. Once you understand the power you have, you can cut the chains which limit your possibilities to a satisfying life. You can do this yourself without the aid of a medical professional, therapist, shaman or other spiritual guide. Memory reshaping is only one way to use your active imagination as an adult, but it is a powerful one. As a child, your reality was more expansive and filled with possibility. As an adult, you can reclaim that almost magical way of viewing reality and also reclaim the innate power you have to free yourself from self-created restrictions of existence. Memory reshaping gives you the opportunity to find out who you can become without the memories which restrain you. Your personal universe is as big as the universe containing all the constellations. It is connected across time and space as a web like your family tree throughout time. Just like your genetic family tree, the tree-like image created by your choices throughout your life are opportunities for restructuring, making different choices, and altering your path.

Memories are merely clay. Reshaping clay before

it becomes hardened in the kiln is a simple thing. Memories remain malleable throughout your life. If you believe some of your memories have become hardened, it is just that, a belief. It is not truth. I challenge you to question your long-held beliefs about memories and to consider that memories are filled with guidance and inspiration as our nightly dreams. You can go back into a dream and uncover its message. You can go back into a memory and reshape it for your benefit. Any imbalance you feel which is connected to a specific memory has the potential to be reshaped, restoring you to wholeness.

You can do this safely without the need to mentally dissect what happened or try and come to some understanding of what it all means. If you think a memory cannot be changed, think again. Reconnecting with your playful mind is not as hard as it may seem. From an early age, you have always been a creator. One of the keys to doing that as an adult is shifting that playful mind to focus internally on your thoughts and memories. It may sound like a cliché to say, but it is like riding a bike; you never forget how. The memories you have are yours. They are not sacred and yet they are. Their sacredness resides in the fact that they have an almost divine power to shift the trajectory of your journey. I believe if you steer clear of memories which can trigger a traumatic event that memory reshaping is a safe tool to enhance your life in any area you wish to create more possibility.

Remember, a memory is a store of energy. The energy it is exacting on your life is indicative as to whether it should be reshaped. The nexus of a memory reveals the possible impact on your life if the energy is released when reshaped. The beauty of memory reshaping is that I created it specifically for myself. This means that you can trust yourself when doing memory reshaping that you may customize it for your own use. Once you have reshaped a memory and tested its impact, you will understand what a powerful tool you now have at your disposal. You will reclaim the playful part of your mind and increase the possibility in your life.

I really did imagine that reshaping a memory would have significant effects on my life. Yet, I had no idea of the revelations which would be forthcoming once the reshaped memory was tested. The insights uncovered seemed to be coming from someplace other than my usual way of perceiving the world and others. I think it is obvious that reshaping releases long hidden energy and potential. I can only imagine what it might do for you if you have the courage to reshape the controlling memories in your life. I challenge you to experiment with other methods, self-created or from other books, if you find reshaping is not your cup of tea.

We all have memories but we each have our individual ways of interacting with the world and each other. Your path may demand a very different way of addressing memories which are limiting your possibilities. Be open to and seek the methods and tools which resonate with who you are and how you are most comfortable navigating the world. Be true to who you are. My prayer for each one of you is to release the pent-up energy you need to become your best self. I wish you all to become your best selves and achieve your most cherished dreams. Bless you on your journey to increased possibility and wholeness.

AFTERWORD

I would be remiss if I did not talk a little bit about active imagination. It was Jung who coined the term active imagination. It came after years of working on his own self-healing and his reconnecting with memories of his playing as a child. After many years of experimenting on himself, he developed a therapeutic method to use on his clients. Although I am using the same term, active imagination, I have a very different definition. Perhaps I should come up with a different phrase. In any case, active imagination as I use it, does have some connection to Jung's term but also some differences. My use of the term is not as a therapeutic method, although I do believe as Jung did that active imagination will redirect or release energy. I believe that active imagination is less a construct of the mind and more of a psychic appendage. When I ask you to take hold of a rope or to grab a pencil, you (without thinking about it) reach with your hand. When you were a child and a friend said, let's play army or let's have a tea party with our dolls, your mind immediately began to create the internal images, ideas, and scenarios without having to think about the how. Your ability with this psychic appendage is innate. It causes you to step into the almost magical realm which allows anything to be possible. Play is how a child engages with the world. It is only after much social training and systematic reshaping of a child's character to be more serious and controlled that this innate ability is almost completely obliterated. Of course, it can be acceptable if you will direct your attentions to art, music, or team sports, but your innate ability to step into the magical realm of a child with no boundaries begins to fade to the point of being forgotten. I remember distinctly going out to my grandfather's backyard to play Tarzan with friends. Long sticks were spears. Although there were no vines to swing from, my friends and I would pretend we were swinging through the trees. Yes, we did have in mind what we had seen on TV watching Johnny Weissmuller, but that is not what we acted out. We created our own jungle. We fashioned our own animals. We invented our own stories. It all happened without a game plan. There was really no discussion, drafting of rules, or laying out a plan with a path to a specific end. During the hours at play, we were in our own self-created reality. It all came from inspiration without thought. This is the innate ability to play which I am asking that you re-engage with to reshape memories. I am asking you to reach with your psychic appendage to reshape a memory as you would reach for a pencil without thinking about it. There is nothing that you need to force. I was Tarzan in my grandfather's backyard. You may have been a queen, superman, a general, a unicorn, or an alien.

Acknowledgments

A very special thanks to the following people who graciously scanned my drafts for misspellings, confusing language, and basic grammar; Ian Nesbitt, Steve Davis, and Light German. Without their patient and wise direction, you might be tossing this book out the window.

Bibliography

Jung on Active Imagination, 1997, Edited and with an Introduction by Joan Chodorow, Princeton University Press, Jung, C.G.

The Memory Illusion: Remembering, Forgetting, and the Science of False Memory, 2017, Random House UK, Dr. Julia Shaw

Your Destiny is Inside You: Be Your Own Guiding Light, 2020, Ana Pat